Daytona 500

by Eric Ethan

Gareth Stevens Publishing
MILWAUKEE

The author wishes to thank Glen Fitzgerald, George Philips, Mary Jo Lindahl, and Juanita Jones for their help and encouragement.

For a free color catalog describing Gareth Stevens Publishing's list of high-quality books and multimedia programs, call 1-800-542-2595 (USA) or 1-800-461-9120 (Canada). Gareth Stevens Publishing's Fax: (414) 225-0377.

Library of Congress Cataloging-in-Publication Data

Ethan, Eric.
    Daytona 500 / by Eric Ethan.
        p. cm. — (NASCAR! an imagination library series)
    Includes index.
    Summary: Discusses the background, events, and rules of the Daytona 500, the most prestigious of the NASCAR Winston Cup racing series.
    ISBN 0-8368-2138-6 (lib. bdg.)
    1. Daytona 500 (Automobile race)—Juvenile literature. [1. Daytona 500 (Automobile race). 2. Stock car racing.] I. Title. II. Series: Ethan, Eric. NASCAR! an imagination library series.
GV1033.5.D39E85   1999
796.72'06'875921—dc21   99-14717

First published in North America in 1999 by
Gareth Stevens Publishing
1555 North RiverCenter Drive, Suite 201
Milwaukee, WI 53212 USA

This edition © 1999 by Gareth Stevens, Inc. Text by Eric Ethan. Photographs © 1998: Cover, pp. 7, 11, 13, 15 - Don Grassman; pp. 5, 17, 19, 21 - Ernest Masche. Illustration: p 9. - The Official NASCAR Preview and Press Guide. Additional end matter © 1999 by Gareth Stevens, Inc.

Text: Eric Ethan
Page layout: Lesley M. White
Cover design: Lesley M. White
Editorial assistant: Diane Laska

Printed in the United States of America

1 2 3 4 5 6 7 8 9 03 02 01 00 99

TABLE OF CONTENTS

Metric Chart
1 mile = 1.609 kilometers
100 miles = 160.9 km
500 miles = 804.5 km

Words that appear in the glossary are printed in
boldface type the first time they occur in the text.

THE DAYTONA 500

The Daytona 500 is the most prestigious event in the National Association for **Stock Car** Auto Racing (NASCAR) Winston Cup racing series. This race has been held every year since 1959. Throughout its history, it has attracted more race fans than any other NASCAR race. The first winner was Lee Petty, father of one of the most famous of all NASCAR drivers, Richard Petty. Richard Petty won the Daytona 500 seven times between 1964 and 1981. This record has never been surpassed. Cale Yarborough holds the next best record, having won four times between 1968 and 1984.

The race is 500 miles long, or 200 laps around the track. Recent winners have averaged about 150 miles per hour, finishing in approximately 3½ hours.

*Bobby Labonte leads the pack coming out of a **banked** turn onto the flat straightaway at the 1998 Daytona 500.*
CIA Stock Photo: Ernest Masche

DAYTONA INTERNATIONAL SPEEDWAY

The Daytona 500 is held the first week in February at the Daytona International Speedway in Daytona, Florida. William H. G. France, Sr., opened the racetrack in 1959. He is considered to be the founder of NASCAR. In 1947, he arranged the first NASCAR organizational meeting in Daytona.

The 110,500 permanent seats at Daytona are completely sold out during major races. While the Daytona 500 gets the most attention, many other racing events are held there each year, such as the Pepsi 400, superbike racing, and the World Karting Association races. Daytona International Speedway hosts the most diverse schedule of racing on the globe, earning it the title "World Center of Racing." It is home to the "World Center of Racing" visitors' center.

The Daytona 500 racetrack is wide enough for three cars to drive side-by-side.
CIA Stock Photo: Don Grassman

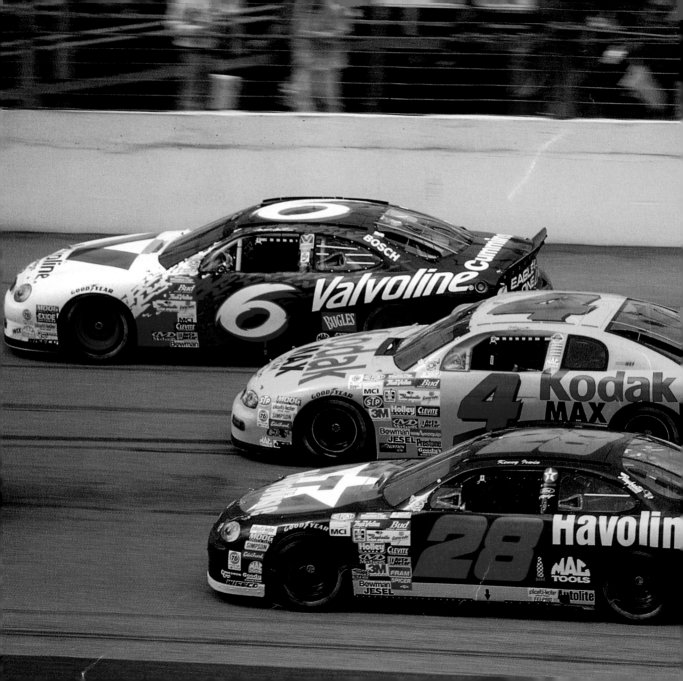

THE TRACK

Daytona International Speedway is a 2.5-mile tri-oval. The term *tri-oval* means the speedway has three turns instead of the two normally found on regular ovals. When the racetrack was built, a large amount of dirt was piled up at the corners to give the track a steep incline of 31 degrees. These are called banked corners. They allow race cars to go around the corners very fast without flying off the track. So much dirt was dug out of the center of the course for the banks that a 44-acre lake called Lake Lloyd was created.

Cars can reach speeds of 220 miles per hour on the back straight. The single-lap record of 210.364 miles per hour was set in 1987 by Bill Elliott. Buddy Baker set the race record in 1980 at 177.602 miles per hour.

Lake Lloyd is located in the middle of the Daytona International Speedway. It was created when dirt was removed and used to build banked corners.
The Official NASCAR Preview and Press Guide

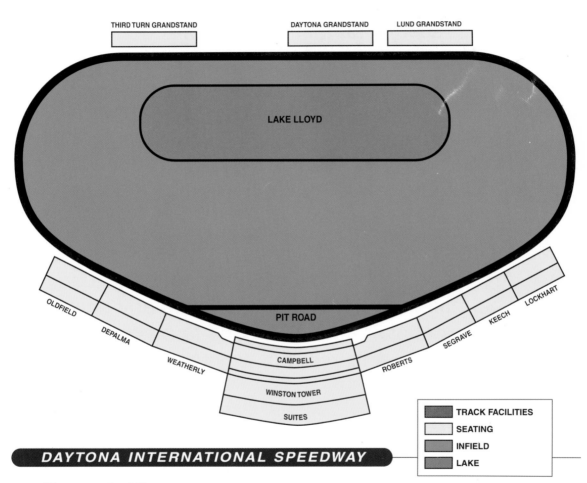

THIRD TURN GRANDSTAND

DAYTONA GRANDSTAND

LUND GRANDSTAND

LAKE LLOYD

PIT ROAD

OLDFIELD

DEPALMA

WEATHERLY

CAMPBELL

WINSTON TOWER

SUITES

ROBERTS

SEGRAVE

KEECH

LOCKHART

	TRACK FACILITIES
	SEATING
	INFIELD
	LAKE

DAYTONA INTERNATIONAL SPEEDWAY

Distance: *2.5 Miles*

Banking: *31 degrees*

Qualifying Record: *Bill Elliott, 210.364 mph (42.783 seconds), set February 9, 1987*

Race Record (500 Miles): *Buddy Baker, 177.602 mph, set February 17, 1980*

NASCAR RACERS

   NASCAR racers look a little like new-model **sedans**. They are very different from regular cars, however. They don't have doors or trunks that open — drivers must crawl in and out through a window. A very powerful motor is placed into a lightweight frame. There is one seat for the driver, who is surrounded by a padded steel roll cage that protects him in case of an accident.

   Motors are specially modified factory stock motors. NASCAR has rules that limit what racing teams can do to their motors. The goal is to prevent any team from having an unfair advantage and to make the driver's skill an essential part of winning races.

Mark Martin drove car number six in the 1998 Daytona 500 race.
CIA Stock Photo: Don Grassman

11

Race cars reach very high speeds. Special tires help hold them on the track. The cars get the best traction and handling, however, through the downward force created by air traveling over the tops of the cars at high speed.

Air rushing under cars as they go around the track can make the racers fly into the air and crash. If you look closely at a NASCAR race car, you will see a low wraparound bumper on the front. This is called an **air dam**. It pushes the air around to the sides of the car. On the trunk of the car is a flat piece of metal that sticks up at an angle. This is called a **spoiler**. Air hits the spoiler when the car is traveling at high speed and pushes the back end down.

Notice the steep bank that is an important feature of the Daytona International Speedway.
CIA Stock Photo: Don Grassman

13

DRIVERS AND TEAMS

Lake Speed drove in the 1998 Daytona race. He has been a professional driver since 1980. During his nineteen-year NASCAR career, he has won nearly $5 million.

At Daytona, Speed's major **sponsor** was the Cartoon Network. The car is owned by Harry Melling. Like every other NASCAR racer, the car Speed drove was covered with sponsors' **logos**. Each sponsor pays money to place a logo on a car. This money helps cover expenses for the car and team.

Lake Speed drove car number nine at Daytona in 1998.
CIA Stock Photo: Don Grassman

15

QUALIFYING

Most NASCAR races allow about forty cars to enter. Each team that wants to compete in the big race must first show how fast its car can go in a **qualifying** lap. The fastest cars earn a position in the main race. Those that post the highest qualifying speeds start the race in front. One-lap speed records are often set during qualifying as drivers try to secure the **pole** position for the start of the race.

Qualifying also gives team mechanics a chance to tune the car to the track. Making adjustments is a constant process.

Drivers Bobby Labonte and Terry Labonte lead the pack out of a banked corner at the 1998 Daytona 500.
CIA Stock Photo: Ernest Masche

RACE DAY

Excitement is everywhere on race day. Over 170,000 fans attend the Daytona 500 each year. The cars line up in qualifying order. Then the **starter** drops the green flag to begin the race. The next three hours require every bit of luck, skill, and speed each driver has.

Winning the races means driving fast — but much more. Cars race closely together at high speed. Avoiding a race-ending accident is a real challenge. Drivers must also determine when they need to make a **pit stop** for fuel, new tires, or minor repairs. Cars battle back and forth for the lead the entire race. In 1996, Dale Jarrett won the Daytona 500, but he was only a few seconds ahead of second-place winner Dale Earnhardt.

Drivers Darrell Waltrip and Steve Park slide past a damaged car after colliding in the 1998 Daytona 500.
CIA Stock Photo: Ernest Masche

ACTION IN THE PITS

Pit crews service the cars during the race. In the past, pit crews communicated with drivers using chalkboard signs. Two-way radios are now used.

Even the best drivers have to stop for fuel and new tires. Tires built for high speeds and hot track surfaces are used by all teams, but the tires quickly wear out during races. There are even special tires made for traction on wet courses. Every driver worries about mechanical problems. Pit crew mechanics can help win races by quickly fixing whatever problem occurs during a race. Obviously, the quicker the car is in and out of the pit, the better its chances of winning.

Dale Jarrett's pit crew is one of the best in all of NASCAR racing.
CIA Stock Photo: Ernest Masche

21

RACE SAFETY

In the early days of racing, fans sat very close to the tracks. When cars lost control and had accidents, however, fans could be injured. Modern tracks are specially designed for safety. At Daytona International, most seating is on the straightaways, where cars are less likely to leave the track. The grandstands are built above the track behind special walls and fences designed to catch any cars or debris that may leave the track.

Drivers know racing is a dangerous sport. They take a lot of precautions, such as wearing fire-retardant clothes and driving cars containing a steel roll cage, fire extinguisher, and an emergency air supply. The most important safety factor is still each driver's skill.

GLOSSARY

You can find these words on the pages listed. Reading a word in a sentence helps you understand it even better.

air dam — the front bumper on a car that pushes air to the sides of the car 12

banked — inclined upward from the inside edge 8, 9

logos (LOW-gos) — graphic designs that feature the name or product of a company 14

pit stop — a time-out when a car goes to the side of the track where team members attend to it 18

pole — the inside, front spot in a car race 16

qualifying (KWAH-lih-fy-ing) — a test that makes a person or object fit for a certain position 9, 16

sedans (seh-DANS) — cars with two or four doors and both front and rear seats 10

spoiler (SPOY-ler) — a flat piece of metal on the trunk of a car that pushes the back end of the car down 12

sponsor (SPON-ser) — a business that financially supports something, such as a race car 14

starter — a person who signals the beginning of a race 18

stock car — a new-model sedan manufactured by Detroit automakers, such as Ford, General Motors, and Chevrolet 4

PLACES TO WRITE

International Motor Sports Museum
Public Relations Manager
3198 Speedway Boulevard
Talladega, AL 35160

Daytona USA
Public Relations Manager
1801 West International Boulevard
Daytona Beach, FL 32114

Motorbooks International
Public Relations Manager
729 Prospect Avenue/Box 1
Osceola, WI 54020

John Story, Director of Public Relations
Daytona International Speedway
P.O. Box 2801
Daytona Beach, FL 32120

WEB SITES

www.nascar.com

This is the official web site of the National Association for Stock Car Auto Racing.

www.ciastockphoto.com

This is one of the best NASCAR photo sites. It is the source of many of the pictures in this book. It presents new images during each racing season.

racing.yahoo.com/rac/nascar

At this web site, race fans can find current NASCAR race results, standings, schedules, driver profiles, feature stories, and merchandise.

Due to the dynamic nature of the Internet, some web sites stay current longer than others. To find additional web sites, use a reliable search engine with one or more of the following keywords: *Daytona 500, Daytona International Speedway, Dale Earnhardt, William H. G. France, Sr., Dale Jarrett, Lake Lloyd, NASCAR, Lee Petty, Richard Petty, Lake Speed,* and *World Center of Racing.*

INDEX

DEMCO